CW01025278

nIVAnnotations
6

STUART HALL AND SARAT MAHARAJ
MODERNITY AND DIFFERENCE

FOREWORD BY GILANE TAWADROS

EDITED BY SARAH CAMPBELL AND GILANE TAWADROS

institute of international visual arts

On the cover:
Pavel Braila, *Recalling Events*, 2000
Recalling Events was a performance that
took place at the Jan Van Eyck Akademie
in Maastricht. Writing in four languages –
Romanian, Russian, French and English –
Braila records on a blackboard significant
events from his past, expressing his
emotional response to them in the present
day. He attempts to erase each event as
soon as he has written about it, but the
chalk sticks to his body as a constant
reminder of his past. As the performance
continues, both Braila and the blackboard
become increasingly smeared in the chalk
that has been used to write the artist's
own history.

Published in the United Kingdom by the
Institute of International Visual Arts
(inIVA), 2001

Institute of International Visual Arts
6-8 Standard Place
Rivington Street
London EC2A 3BE
www.iniva.org

Texts © 2001, the authors

Any copy of this book issued by the
publisher as a paperback is sold subject to
the condition that it shall not by way of
trade or otherwise be lent, resold, hired out
or otherwise circulated without the
publisher's prior consent in any form of
binding or cover other than that in which it
is published and without a similar condition
including these words being imposed on a
subsequent purchaser.

All rights reserved. No part of this
publication may be reproduced or
transmitted in any form or by any means,
electronic or mechanical, including
photocopy, recording or any other
information storage and retrieval
system, without prior permission in
writing from the publisher.

ISBN 1 899846 30 1
A catalogue record of this book is available
from the British Library

Edited by Sarah Campbell
and Gilane Tawadros
Designed by Maria Beddoes and Paul Khera,
assisted by Scott Lee Cash
Printed by Spiderweb in the UK

Preface

There was an overwhelming response to the 'Modernity and Difference' discussion that the Institute of International Visual Arts (inIVA) organised at the Lux Cinema in Hoxton, London, on 25 October 2000. It was hardly surprising in view of the stature of the two speakers, Professor Stuart Hall and Professor Sarat Maharaj, and the contribution that they have made to some of the most pressing cultural and political issues of our time.

The discussion was the final instalment in a series of exhibitions and events that inIVA organised over the summer of 2000 under the heading of *Modern*. The season interrogated the way in which we define what it is to be modern; it asked whether modernity is rooted in a particular time and location or, alternatively, whether it can be perceived as a way of thinking, living and working.

The discussion was intended to be an informal conversation around questions of modernity and difference, questions that both Sarat Maharaj and Stuart Hall have engaged with in different contexts over a number of years. They are also questions which, in one way or another, lie at the heart of inIVA. The subject of the conversation is all the more relevant given that both men have played an important role in the conception and development of inIVA, as architects of the intellectual and creative framework for the organisation.

In his keynote address to a conference, held at the Tate Gallery in May 1999, entitled 'Museums of Modern Art and the End of History', Stuart Hall challenged the assumption embedded in the practices of the European museum that modernism is the property of Western Europe and contended that:

...the world is absolutely littered by modernities and by practising artists, who never regarded modernism as the secure possession of the West, but perceived it as a language which was both open to them but which they would have to transform. The history therefore should now be rewritten as a set of cultural translations rather than as a universal movement which can be located securely within a culture, within a history, within a space, within a chronology and within a set of political and cultural relations.[1]

The full text of Stuart Hall's keynote address has been published here since it maps out the relationship between modernism, modernity and difference and throws down the gauntlet to us all to reconsider the history of modernity and modernism as it has been enshrined in the Western canon. It opens it up from a singular historical and geographical space to a series of fluid, heterogeneous, cultural formations, or 'cultural translations'.

Questions of translation and untranslatability were first broached by Sarat Maharaj's text, 'Perfidious Fidelity: The Untranslatability of the Other' in *Global Visions*, the publication that brings together papers from inIVA's first conference held in 1994 to debate the possibility of a 'new internationalism':

In the contemporary scene of cultural mix and swap, translation is about unending production of difference — spasmic, unforeseeable transformation. This has to be distinguished from the view of difference as diversity — a spectrum of fixed, unchanging markers of cultural difference — which by the 1990s has increasingly come to be associated with official multicultural strategies. The latter is concerned mainly with the regulation and management of difference.[2]

In the discussion between Stuart Hall and Sarat Maharaj, they sketch out a radical new philosophical framework for the understanding of identity and difference that disturbs the logic of 'official multiculturalism' and its concern with the regulation and management of difference, or what Sarat Maharaj calls 'multicultural managerialism'. Without a pure beginning or origin, identities and cultures are to be understood, Stuart Hall argues as 'an infinite, incomplete series of translations'.

The ensuing debate encompasses a vast array of issues and questions moving from the theoretical, visual and linguistic spaces through to the arena of the social and political realities. In discussing the irresistible 'multicultural drift' occurring in Europe, Stuart Hall warns that the rise of multiculturalism has been accompanied by a parallel rise in racism and racial violence. The question therefore remains: Is there some way of learning to live with difference?

Gilane Tawadros
Director, inIVA

Notes
1. Stuart Hall, keynote address, 'Museums of Modern Art and the End of History' conference, Tate Gallery, London, May 1999
2. Sarat Maharaj, 'Dislocutions: Interim Entries for a *dictionnaire élémentaire* on Cultural Translation' in *Re-Verberations: Tactics of Resistance, Forms of Agency in Trans/cultural Practices*, edited by Jean Fisher, Jan van Eyck Akademie Editions, 2000

Sarat Maharaj
and Stuart
Hall at the
'Modernity
and
Difference'
discussion at
the Lux
Centre,
Hoxton,
London,
25 October
2000

Museums of Modern Art and the End of History

I have no authority to address this occasion either as an art critic or as a historian – a lack which I find curiously liberating in this distinguished company. I am very involved in some areas of the practice of visual arts in Britain at the moment, as I have the honour to chair the Boards of both the Institute of International Visual Arts (inIVA) and Autograph, the Association of Black Photographers. I therefore know something about the area of contemporary artistic practice which I regard as one of the liveliest, most vigorous and most creative sectors of the contemporary arts anywhere. It might therefore be useful to say something from this non-specialist point of view about what I would call the cultural 'conditions of existence' for the exhibition and production of contemporary art.

I put 'exhibition', out of sequence, first because the question of the museum is foregrounded in the conference title; and I use the expression 'cultural conditions of existence' in the specific sense that all important practices, art practices included, always have prior conditions of existence. 'Conditions of existence' are different from the notion of a determining force, in the strong sense of determinacy. Conditions do not determine either the form or the content or, indeed, the tendency and direction of a practice, but nevertheless without conditions of existence, a practice could not exist. A practice is always a labour – a 'work' – on pre-existing materials and traces. Conditions therefore have a bearing on how those practices are actually executed in the world. Those who in a professional capacity are specifically related to judging, assessing and exhibiting the results of a practice come high in the pecking order and those who are actually producing the work come highest of all – though they are not always accorded the status and rewards they deserve – which leaves me as a lowly handmaiden in this operation. But I want to pick out certain aspects of these conditions of existence for contemporary art and, in a simple way, relate them to the themes and questions signalled in the title.

Rather than 'Museums of Modern Art and the End of History', I am tempted to suggest that the title of this conference should be 'The End of Museums of Modern Art and the Beginning of History'. We could learn a great deal simply by reversing all the terms. What I want to talk about is exactly the sort of 'ending' signalled by that kind of reversal. Of course, it would be too easy to think that simply turning all the terms of a dominant paradigm upside down will help us to understand what is going on. In that sense, I am not interested in endings; instead, I am going to talk about 'turns'. The idea of museums in general, but also museums of modern art, is in trouble as a result of certain deep historical shifts or 'turns': transformations of theory and consciousness, but also shifts in the actual cultural landscape itself.

This 'crisis', if we may call it that, is the cumulative effects of a rather dispersed set of developments – what I refer to as a series of turns - which constitute the end of certain ideas of the museum, of the modernity of modern art and, indeed, of history. That notion of a turn is important for me. A turn is neither an ending nor a reversal; the process continues in the direction in which it was travelling before, but with a critical break, a deflection. After the turn, all of the terms of a paradigm are not destroyed; instead, the deflection shifts the paradigm in a direction which is different from that which one might have presupposed from the previous moment. It is not an ending, but a break, and the notion of breaks – of ruptures and of turns – begins to provide us with certain broad handles with which to grasp the current crisis of modernity, and thus of the museums of the modern.

This is clearly related to the much abused notion of the 'post', which has already been referred to, so I must spend a moment dogmatically reiterating what 'post' means to me. I do not use the term to mean 'after' in a sequential or chronological sense, as though one phase or epoch or set of practices has ended and an absolutely new one is beginning. Post, for me, always refers to the aftermath or the after-flow of a particular configuration. The impetus which constituted one particular historical or aesthetic moment disintegrates in the form in which we know it. Many of

those impulses are resumed or reconvened in a new terrain or context, eroding some of the boundaries which made our occupation of an earlier moment seem relatively clear, well bounded and easy to inhabit, and opening in their place new gaps, new interstices.

Let us look at three examples. The post-colonial is not the ending of colonialism but is what happens after the end of the national independence movement. All those contradictions and problems which constituted the dependency of colonial societies are reconvened, partly now within the old colonised societies, but also inside the metropolis, which was previously regarded as standing outside of this process. Similarly, post-structuralism spends all its time and energies saying how it is an advance on structuralism, and yet the first thing to recognise is that, without structuralism, post-structuralism could not exist. It continues in its bloodstream, but in a disseminated or deconstructed form, which allows the original structuralist impulse, transformed, to take on new directions. I think the term 'post-modern' is exactly the same.

I do not want to evoke any of the enormous rubbish that has been talked about under the title of 'post-modernism', but instead want to focus on the kernel of significance in the term once it has been stripped of some of its many accretions. It seems to me that 'the modern' has ceased to be an ever-increasing present form or state of existence and is becoming a moment in history. When that happens, our understanding shifts from an awareness of the ground on which a practice stands to seeing where it came from, how it evolved and this enables us to ask the question: 'What might come after it, 'post' it?'

F. N. Souza,
*Two Saints in
a Landscape*,
1961

There has always been something contradictory about the relationship between modernity and history, which is bound to problematise the notion of art history itself. Art history has given the museum its principles of organisation, providing the practices of curating, exhibiting, collecting and classification with a scholarly ground. The historicisation, therefore, of what was previously perceived as an entirely new historical moment inevitably leads to a sense of operating in a gap between a past which is not quite over and a future which has not yet started (and may never happen in the totalised form in which we imagine it). Writing the history of a phenomenon or of a movement or of an epoch does, in a very complex way, suggest that one can trace its genealogy – what its evolution has been, define the principle forces which will drive it forward and ask the question of whether it has a conclusion. But this historicising tendency is seen as contradictory in the context of modernity, since modernity was precisely a fundamental rupture with 'the past' in that sense. It was a break into contingency and, by contingency, I do not mean complete absence of pattern, but a break from the established continuities and connections which made artistic practice intelligible in a historical review. It focused as much on the blankness of the spaces between things as on the things itself and on the excessive refusal of continuities. It was always caught between the attempt, on the one hand, to turn the sign back to a kind of direct engagement with material reality and, on the other, to set the sign free of history in a proliferating utopia of pure forms. Writing histories of modernity is not impossible, but I think they have always been extremely difficult to suture back into the more confident historical organisation of the history of Western art, which extends roughly from the Renaissance until the modern itself. I think we have reached the death of that idea of the modern, the logic of whose architecture, T.J.B. Clark (*Farewell to an Idea. Episodes from a History of Modernism*, 1999) argues, we can no longer intuitively grasp.

I want to talk instead about the turn from modernism, but using 'turn' in the sense I have already established. Let me return to that version of post-modernism, which cites modernism as if the entire modern movement can be condensed forwards to the point of its elaboration under the aegis of American art and architecture – the 'American' moment. The notion of modernism which reads as if it came to its apotheosis only at its very end seems to me to misunderstand, misread and grossly oversimplify the radical, aesthetic, social and cultural impulses which made modernism the dynamic movement that it was. American cultural critics have a great deal to answer for by trying to subsume the many modernisms under the aegis of what we might call the age of the American empire.

It seems that something significant has to be taken on board about the persistence of the impulse of modernity itself within post-modernism. I cite three examples. The first is what I would call modernism in the streets. I think post-modernism is best described as precisely that; it is the end of modernism *in the museum* and the penetration of the modernist ruptures into everyday life, which is closely related to my second example, the aestheticisation of daily life. This might puzzle people in this room who think of contemporary life as the very antithesis of the aesthetic, but personally I think the symbolic has never had such a wide

significance as it does in contemporary life. In earlier theories, the symbolic was corralled into a narrow terrain, but it has now entirely imploded in terms of late-modern experience and we find the languages of the aesthetic as appropriate within popular culture or public television, as they are within the most *recherché* rooms of the Museum of Modern Art. There are aesthetic practices distributed by a massive cultural industry on a global scale and the aesthetic is, indeed, the bearer of some of the most powerful impulses in modern culture as a whole, including what we used to think of as its antithesis – the 'new economy' which is, par excellence, a *cultural* economy. This notion of a modernism that is to be found inscribed on the face of everyday life, in everyday fashion, in popular culture and in the popular media, in consumer culture and the visual revolution, does obviously jeopardise the whole concept of gathering together the best of all this in one place and calling it 'a museum'.

Alongside all of this is my third example, the proliferation of media or, in other words, the means of signification. I read recently that it is completely ridiculous to define modern contemporary visual art practices in terms of the media in which they are executed; instead, we must consider the proliferation of sites and places in which the modern artistic impulse is taking place, in which it is encountered and seen. This is not just a reservation about the white cube gallery space. This is an explosion of the boundaries – the symbolic as well as physical and material limits – within which the notion of art and aesthetic practices have been organised. Young intellectuals – barely able to spell intellectual, let alone call themselves that – who are working somewhere within the cultural industries, with visual languages, are as deeply and profoundly implicated in the breaking point of modern artistic practices as the most fully paid-up members of the most academic, scholarly schools of art. That they came in through the back door and went out into industry is not important. What is relevant, however, is the proliferation of these practices and the degree to which this proliferation sits most uncomfortably with the prestige attached to the process which attempts to sift, on some universal criteria of historical value, the best that is being produced and gets it displayed inside some well-patrolled set of walls. Modernism in the streets, the aestheticisation of everyday life and the proliferation of sites and means of signification are some ways of re-reading post-modernism, or the post-modern 'turn', as the aftermath of modernism.

Post-modernism is not a new movement that kicked modernism into touch, but, instead, by building on and breaking from modernism, it transformed it by taking it out into the world. Similarly, we might talk about the post-museum – not in the sense of the necessary end of all museums, but in terms of the radical transformation of the museum as a concept. I would call it the *relativisation* of the museum, which can now be perceived as only one site among many in the circulation of aesthetic practices. It is certainly true that the museum remains a very privileged, well-funded site, which is still closely tied to the accumulation of cultural capital, of power and prestige, but in terms of the real understanding of how artistic practices proliferate in our society, it is only one site and no longer enjoys the privileged position that it had historically.

Now I want to look at what one might call 'post-history'. In exactly the same way that I have been talking about the post-modern, post-history is not the end of history. In fact, some of the most important critical and theoretical developments have arisen from the greater historicisation of aesthetic practices, which we have tended to talk of as if they were universal. The historicising function has not therefore gone away; but History, with a capital 'H', which is now increasingly understood as one grand narrative among many narratives, has managed to situate itself, or substitute itself, in the place of the Universal. The history around which the practices of the arts have organised and ordered themselves is the lifeblood of the museum's self-understanding and opens connections which I find so delicate and impossible to understand that I only cite them. There is an almost impossibly refined and elaborated exchange between history and value, which you might think are antithetical terms – after all, if something was important in a particular period, it is highly unlikely that it will be important in all other periods – and yet value reaches for a universal horizon from within a deeper and more profound sense of historical understanding.

In what sense then, do we have a post-history? Firstly we should be aware that histories *are* narratives and that accordingly we have histories rather than a singular history. These narratives are a discursive imposition of beginnings, middles and, indeed, endings on to histories which do not naturally produce themselves in this convenient form. Therefore, we are not talking about the history of art, but about how we have chosen to narrate the identity of the histories of art to ourselves; the notion of narrative has interrupted and deflected the purity of the historical impulse.

Li Yuan-chia, studio exhibition (detail), Boothby, Cumbria, 1968

There has been a similar deflection from what I would call history to culture – the 'cultural turn'. If you think of the historical as having

always provided the context within which art historians and critics sought to embed particular practices and texts, then I think we have seen an increase in the use of the notion of cultural context, which of course has historical overtones. At the same time, it seems that there has been an important shift from being interested simply in the historical context of a text or an artist or a practice to embracing its cultural conditions of existence. This destroys or subverts the traditional work and its context approach, which has underwritten art historical understanding for so long. It has to do with what one might call the spatialisation of time, which is a prominent feature or phenomenon of a contemporary sensibility.

In terms of post-histories, it is the cogency and compulsiveness of evolutionary explanations which have been broken down, that is to say explanations which trace continuities and look at traditions as unbroken, as unfolding webs of influence, trailing from one moment to another. We have been alerted, not to the absence of traditions (plural), but to the inhabitation of traditions – particularly for where they break and for where they turn back on or away from themselves and on to something else. Tradition must be understood as a discursive field. There is always something of *the present* at stake in how it is inhabited. We are more aware of constituting the discursive ground on which histories have to be constructed as the difficult ground which enables us to connect this to that or this particular text to that particular work. Talking about the history of a practice, of an artist, of a body of work or of a text, as it is read and re-read from one moment to another, simply does not support that organic evolutionary conception of the historical or indeed of tradition, genre or convention – the staples of the museum's self-understanding. I am not suggesting that this approach has not had profound pay-offs for art history and for critical understanding, but I am talking about it more as a space which the modern sensibility can no longer inhabit with confidence in the old way. It can no longer rest there in the knowledge of having found a scholarly and evaluative foundational ground from which to organise and classify the objects of a particular collection.

Gavin Jantjes, *Untitled*, 1989

The next 'post' that I wanted to talk about is what I want to call post-culture. You will say there is nothing post about culture; it is the ever-present, ever-evolving signifier of our times. Everybody is interested in it, the prime minister most of all; whenever you offer him an institution which seems resilient to reform, he says we need a 'culture change'. So culture is the ground on which everybody is somehow now said to be operating. But what is entailed in this conception of culture? We can no longer inhabit a notion of culture

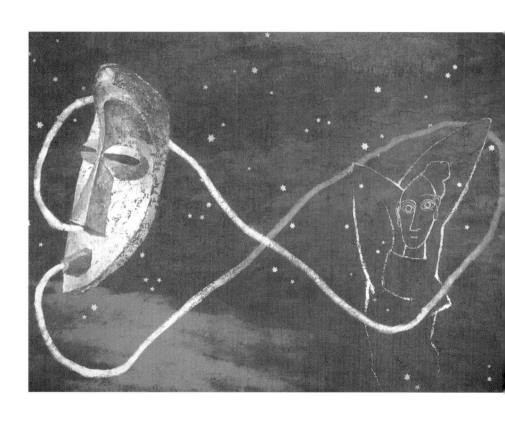

in the old anthropological sense, as something which is clearly bounded, internally self-sufficient and relatively homogenous across its members, which sustains and regulates individual conduct within the framework that it offers. Cultures, in that anthropological sense of specifically defined ways of life, have been broken into and interrupted by cosmopolitan dispersals, by migration and displacement. I think that the collapse of that anthropological definition – culture as a way of life – has to do with the point at which the West began to universalise itself. It is connected with the attempt to construct the world as a single place, with the world market, with globalisation and with that moment when Western Europe tried to convert the rest of the world into a province of its own forms of life. From that moment onwards – the moment of modernity – we could no longer think in terms of cultures which are integral, organic, whole, which are well bounded spatially, which support us and which write the scripts of our lives from start to finish. The ending of this moment of Euro-centric closure and its panoptic project has been a long and protracted one, but it has been increasingly prized open.

The movement from an anthropological to a signifying conception of culture does not mean that cultures become less important. Instead, we are now talking more than ever before about the domain, the importance and the proliferation of meanings by which people live their lives, understand and contest where they are and develop aesthetic and artistic forms of expression. What has disappeared is the ability to carve those forms of expressions into strictly classificatory boxes, so that the primitive and the ancient fit like two rooms inside the modern, with the modern itself boxed inside the ancient. The modern has been inside the primitive and the ancient since 1492 roughly speaking, so what is this 'new' discovery that all of a sudden there are more than one set of modernities? They have been proliferating ever since the world began, only ever tentatively, unevenly, contradictorily, to be convened under the rubric of Western time. This does not mean that we are merely moving everywhere towards a cloning of the West. Instead, those sharp distinctions which underpin our classification – that fixed notion of primordial cultural difference – between tradition and modernity simply do not explain any longer the way in which individuals and their practices are *both* embedded in certain cultural languages or repertoires and at the same time reach across any frontiers which they construct to those which lie beyond – the phenomenon of vernacular cosmopolitanism which is globalisation's accompanying shadow. This is nothing other than the shift from the notion of difference as an either/or concept to Derrida's notion of *differance,* in which you cannot make an absolute distinction between a here and a there, inside and outside.

The history of the relationship between the West and its others is a history of the transformations which have changed both out there and here. It is true that these changes are more dramatic under the conditions of modern globalisation, in which, undeniably, a lot of out there is actually in here now and vice versa. They are in here, trying to become like you, but also making you different, more like them in their *differance.*

The idea that we live in a well-bounded, well-policed, well-frontiered set of spaces, in which you can move from this room to that, tracing how that became this and how the practices governed by a particular culture evolved to become something different, simply misses the degree to which cultures can no longer be clearly categorised. With the modern and even the post-modern condition, the process of *cultural translation* means that cultural languages are not closed; they are constantly transformed from both within and outside, continuously learning from other languages and traditions, drawing them in and producing something which is irreducible to either of the cultural elements which constituted it in the first place. The most dramatic example of how the notion of cultural translation is the only way in which the cultural process today can be properly grasped is found in the history of modernism itself. The latter has been written precisely as if modernism was a set of triumphal artistic practices, located in what you might think of as the West. However, a small number of deracinated artists out there were drawn to this pole of attraction and did relate to it, but of course, in the dominant way the history is read, they cannot be considered to have contributed in any central way to the history and evolution of modernist art practices. In reality, the world is absolutely littered by modernities and by practising artists, who never regarded modernism as the secure possession of the West, but perceived it as a language which was both open to them but which they would have to transform. The history therefore should now be rewritten as a set of cultural translations rather than as a universal movement which can be located securely within *a* culture, within *a* history, within *a* space, within *a* chronology and within *a* set of political and cultural relations.

The final 'post' I would like to talk about has to do with the question of the post-West. In the light of what I said earlier, we are aware that modern museums of art and other kinds of museums now function in the context of a widening and expanding process of

globalisation, which is often seen from within the West as a kind of inevitable homogenisation; it is as if unfortunately everybody in the world is determined, predetermined, to end up looking like 'us'. In that sense, the process is sometimes referred to as the 'end of history', but I do not believe it is. If you think about contemporary forms of globalisation – which are of course driven by Western technology, by Western capital on a global scale and by the flows of international finance which has the capacity to undermine societies far removed from ours by the proliferation of the cultural industry – then I quite understand that a dynamic exists, which is grounded and rooted in the development and over-development of the West. However, I think that its actual impact on the rest of the world has not been simply to homogenise it, but also to expose it to differentiation. The impulse of 'difference' operating in and across the world is, to me, as powerful and as unintended a consequence of capitalist globalisation and modernity as the impulse towards the McDonaldsisation of the world. I do not believe any law of history exists which will guarantee that the one must prevail over the other, although I recognise the grim unevenness and contradictoriness of what we may call the 'global balance of social forces'.

If we look at the way in which contemporary art practices locate themselves within an awareness of the slow decentring of the West, we see the constitution of lateral relations in which the West is an absolutely pivotal, powerful, hegemonic force, but is no longer the only force within which creative energies, cultural flows and new ideas can be concerted. The world is moving outwards and can no longer be structured in terms of the centre/periphery relation. It has to be defined in terms of a set of interesting centres, which are both different from and related to one another. Inhabiting this uneven language of a more common planetary or cosmopolitan consciousness – and I know that this process of globalisation is one which has enormous inequalities built into it – is a deeply and profoundly unequal process. This does not necessarily mean that the game is already so wrapped up that we can designate it with the term 'the end of history'. Any museum which thinks it can incorporate or grasp the best texts and productions of modern artistic practice, believing the world is still organised in a centre/periphery model, simply does not understand the contradictory tensions which are in play. On the one hand are all those lines of force which continue to draw energy, resources, exhibitions and circulation to a very narrow metropolitan centre and, on the other, is the disseminating force of what is happening laterally. On the edge of our consciousness, we are aware that

David
Medalla,
Cloud Gates,
1994

some of the most 'modern' artists are practising in the most 'underdeveloped' places. The account of what matters in the artistic world, from the point of view of the declining, diminishing cultural authority of the West, is expanding in its potential to gobble up everything and yet this is not happening.

If you think about where important movements are being made, sometimes they happen in the centre, but the most exciting artists are those who live simultaneously in the centre and at the periphery. In terms of the conditions of consciousness within which these people start to make artistic practices, they inhabit a world which is torn, on the one hand, by the centralising force of Western modernity, with all the goodies it entails, and, on the other, by the dissemination and proliferation of notions of what it would be like to be vernacular and modern. We are embarking on a hundred different ideas of 'the modern', not one, and therefore, of a thousand practising modern artists, who require recognition within the terms of the criteria that we have stitched into our museum space. Is that the end of the museum? I do not believe it is.

Museums have to understand their collections and their practices as what I can only call 'temporary stabilisations'. What they are – and they must be specific things or they have no interest – is as much defined by what they are not. Their identities are determined by their constitutive outside; they are defined by what they lack and by their other. The relation to the other no longer operates as a dialogue of paternalistic apologetic disposition. It has to be aware that it is a narrative, a selection, whose purpose is not just to disturb the viewer but to itself be disturbed by what it can not be, by its necessary exclusions. It must make its own disturbance evident so that the viewer is not entrapped into the universalised logic of thinking whereby because something has been there for a long period of time and is well funded, it must be 'true' and of value in some aesthetic sense. Its purpose is to destabilise its own stabilities. Of course, it has to risk saying, 'This is what I think is worth seeing and preserving', but it has to turn its criteria of selectivity inside out so that that the viewer becomes aware of both the frame and what is framed.

The viewer should be able to read a particular narrative in the context of other narratives and understand that its identity is always positional. The museum of modern art has a history, a space, a funding, a tradition; it speaks a language but knows that it is no longer the only language in the world. This is a difficult exercise

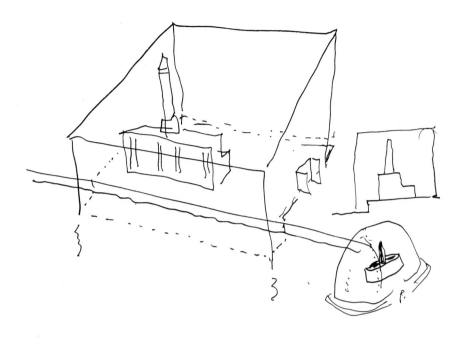

Cedric Price,
*Proposal for
the Tate
Modern*, 1990s

Overleaf:
Aubrey Williams,
*Quartet no. 5,
opus 92*, 1981

because museums, in spite of what we would like to think, are deeply enmeshed in systems of power and privilege. They are locked into the narrowest circulation of art in its diminishing terms and are consequently locked into mindsets which have been institutionalised in those circuits. The process of breaking free is likely to be a long and nasty business. But it can not be long before museums of modern art come to look more and more like what the architect Cedric Price in the recent show at inIVA described as 'cultural centres', characterised by 'calculated uncertainty and conscious incompleteness'.

Stuart Hall

This keynote address was given at the 'Museums of Modern Art and the End of History' conference at the Tate Gallery, London, May 1999

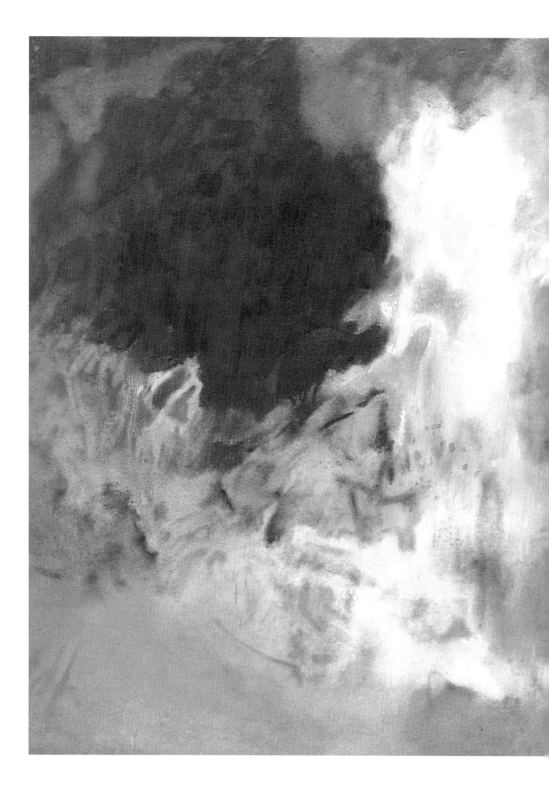

Perfidious Fidelity

The Untranslatability
of the Other

27.4.'94 From Apartheid's dying grip, gently, gently ease the idea it turned against us with such murderous force — 'the untranslatable other'

28.4.'94 The funeral pyre's torched. Speak the idea differently now — for those who survived and those who didn't?

These are rather rough-grained sketch notes towards 'recoding the international' — a task both massive and daunting. My focus is essentially on two things:

1. To move towards reindexing the international space which I should like to describe as the 'scene of translations'. Beyond the demand for assimilation, beyond absolutist notions of difference and identity, beyond the reversible stances of 'self and other' in which the Eurocentric gaze fashions itself as the other, as the intoxicating exotic as in the heady stuff of a Smirnoff ad — in the 1990s, we have come to see the international space as the meeting ground for a multiplicity of tongues, visual grammars and styles. These do not so much translate into one another as translate to produce difference. Have we been all too affirmative about this difference-producing space? How might it be recoded in the light of a more inflected concept of translation? In everyday terms, we see translation as the business of imperceptibly passing through from one language to another, not unlike stacking panes of glass one on top of another, a matter of sheer transparency. But is it no less about taking the measure of the untranslatable, about groping along and clawing at dividing walls, about floundering in an opaque stickiness? This might seem like flying in the face of our workaday

notions of translation. Yet words and images as much mimic as stand off from and pull faces at one another. How therefore to recode translation taking on board ideas about its limits and dead-ends, its impossibility,[1] the notion of the untranslatable, what we might call 'the untranslatability of the term other'?

2.   My second focus is on trying to recode what the scene of translations throws up — hybridity — to recharge it in a double-turn, a positive and negative force in one go. On the one hand, the idea is to see it as a creative force: since each language seems to have its own system and manner of meaning, the construction of meaning in one does not square with that of another. From their very opacity to each other, from in-between them, translation thus cooks up and creates something different, something hybrid. On the other hand, the idea is to ask if the hybrid might not also be seen as the product of translation's failure, as something that falls short of the dream-ideal of translation as a 'transparent' passage from one idiom to another, from self to other.

Two issues, therefore, need to be explored. Is there a danger of hybridity — made-up lingo and style or visual Esperanto — becoming the privileged, prime term, a danger of its swapping places with the notion of stylistic purity? Is it heading towards operating as a catch-all category in which we lump together as diverse works as those of Yasumasa Morimura, Jamelie Hassan, Huang Yong Ping, Doris Salcedo, Vivan Sundaram, Vuyile Cameron Voyiya, Lani Maestro, Sue Williamson and Rasheed Araeen? With this, hybridity — vehicle for demarcating and disseminating difference — seems paradoxically to flip over into its opposite, to function as the label of flattening sameness, as 'new international gothic'. At stake is staving off the tendency for hybridity to settle down into a one-dimensional concept, into what Gayatri Spivak speaks of as 'translatese'[2] — what we might liken to bureaucratese or officialese. The concern is with safeguarding its volatile tension, its force as a double-voicing concept. A recoding would need to affirm its bright and cloudy dimensions — the fact that it is at once the 'success' of translation and its 'failure': that it marks the site of an unceasing tussle between something hard won out of opacity and the impossibility of transparency.

The notion of 'untranslatability' was given a singular twist by Apartheid for its own ends. It projected the impossibility of

27

translation, of transparency, to argue that self and other could never translate into or know each other. This sense of opacity served to underpin its doctrine of an absolute 'epistemic barrier' — grounds for institutionalising a radical sense of ethnic and cultural difference and separateness. Self and other were deemed to be locked in their own discrete, pure spaces. Recoiling from Apartheid's 'pessimistic', violating scripting and staging of the untranslatable, the drive has been to promote hybridity as its 'optimistic' flip side — as the triumph over untranslatability. How to recharge 'hybridity' so that it is prised free from this oppositional coupling? The aim is to prevent it from narrowing down into a reductive, celebratory term. To recode it in more circumspect key involves defining it as a concept that unceasingly plumbs the depths of the untranslatable and that is continually being shaped by that process. It is to reinscribe it with a double-movement that cuts across 'optimism and pessimism, the opaque and the crystal-clear' — to activate it as a play-off between the poles. It amounts to reindexing hybridity as an unfinished, self-unthreading force, even as a concept against itself. At any rate, as an open-ended one that is shot through with memories and intimations of the untranslatable. I have expressed the above in rather clear-cut, decisive terms — in an English kitted out in sturdy, sensible shoes and off on a brisk walk. I should say immediately, however, that it hides much that is undecided, hesitating. For behind the above map lies a vast panic-making searching and exploring that stretches back to my earlier, even more tentative attempts at probing the lines of the inter-cultural 'epistemic barrier'.[3]

Zarina Bhimji, work in progress, 1998–2001

Chohreh
Feyzdjou,
*Boutique
Product of
Chohreh
Feyzdjou*,
1997

Paradoxically, perhaps scandalously, to find solace for my sense of panic and to get to grips with the process of recoding itself, I turned to the *Panic Encyclopedia*, to the section on Panic Hamburgers, skipping over other hair-raising, heebie-jeebie entries.[4]

An ordinary hamburger, as I suppose all of us take for granted — whether diehard or dithering vegan or not — is filled with wholesome chunks of succulent meat. These are, in the *Panic Encyclopedia*'s thinking, metaphors for chunks of nutritious meaning, portions of semantic substance. The Panic Hamburger, on the contrary, devoid of such content, has practically no decent filling to its credit. We might even suspect it of harbouring some sort of synthetic stuff, perhaps even slivers of a textured soya spun mix. At any rate, hardly any semantic substance to sink our teeth into. Except that we might see it in terms of a variety of constructions and recodings: a hamburger for every occasion — for the happy hour or for the blossoming or broken romance. A hamburger constructed as the family afternoon treat or a hamburger for the cranky vegan. I am sure we can agree this has little to do with either McDonalds or other fast-food joints — it's strictly about the process of inscription, erasure and recoding. Are some centuries longer than others? How might we construct and recode the new international century as the longest of them all? — as one that takes in the ancient and modern Jewish diaspora through to the transportation of the enslaved to the Caribbean and US, from the indentured and colonised to the postwar 'dark migrations' and the contemporary scene thick-scribbled with foot and fingerprints of refugees, exiles, deportees. One of Joyce's panic-stricken 100 letter desperation/diasportation words from *Finnegans Wake* evokes it:

Lukkedoerendunandurraskewdylooshooferoyportetooryzoo
ysphalnabortansporthaokansakroidverjkapakkapuk

The word for 'shut door' in six languages, it captures the
unhinging, trapping fear that accompanies the new international
order and its sense of exhilaration, both its closures and
openings. What Joyce hammers out is an unspeakable,
untranslatable Babel word.

Boutique Product of Chohreh Feyzdjou — this is how the exile
artist of Iranian Jewish background bills her work. Framed as
the 'Bazaar of Babel', the installation cites and cancels at
least four acts and scenes of translation. Firstly, it stages
the stereotyped Jewish space — the entrepreneurial scene of
exchange, speculation, transaction. If it marks the still,
traditional sacred space of the Talmudic scroll it is no less the
tumultuous, profane space of buying, selling, shopping and
over-the-counter commerce.

An ashen Auschwitz dust powders the scored, weather-beaten
surfaces — space of the diaspora, deportation, death. Lastly it
stages the Situationists' avant-garde space. Exasperated with
the commodification of art, they had demanded that it be
churned out by the metre in a parody of its commodified fate —
not unlike stacked rolls of cloth and fabric on display. Browsing
through this space one might ask for a metre or two of painting
please. But the translations do not square, each overshoots
the other and is opaque to it. An excess silently dribbles out.
Between the constructions we are left with the remainder of
the untranslatable.

Translation, as Derrida therefore puts it, is quite unlike buying,
selling, swapping — however much it has been conventionally
pictured in those terms. It is not a matter of shipping over juicy
chunks of meaning from one side of the language barrier to the
other — as with fast-food packs at an over-the-counter, take-
away outfit. Meaning is not a readymade portable thing that can
be 'carried over' the divide. The translator is obliged to construct
meaning in the source language and then to figure and fashion it
a second time round in the materials of the language into which he
or she is rendering it.

The translator's loyalties are thus divided and split. He or she has
to be faithful to the syntax, feel and structure of the source

language and faithful to those of the language of translation. We have a clash and collision of loyalties and a lack of fit between the constructions. We face a double writing, what might be described as a 'perfidious fidelity' or, to use Joyce's words, a 'double-cressing' loyalty — tressing, cross-dressing, double-crossing, treacherous. We are drawn into Derrida's 'Babel effect'.

Marcel Duchamp's remarks on the English translation by Richard Hamilton (1960) of his handwritten *Green Box* notes (1912-34) anticipated something of this view of translation. He complimented the English version by noting its 'monstrous veracity' — touching on its skewed fidelities, its truer-than-true unfaithfulness to the original. Referring to the project as a 'crystalline transubstantiation' rather than as a translation — he was to throw together the qualities of sheer transparency against those of the opaque, theological mystery of transformation. His stress is on transmutation — the sense of translation as a semiotic gear-switch, a break from one system of signs and images to another.[5] We might scan the scene of translations taking as its symbol Duchamp's lamp from *Etant Donnés* — the project he secretly worked on from 1946 to 1966. But what more magical a lamp than Aladdin's — which touches on the processes of translation as transmutation and transformation rather than as transfer. The word Aladdin — pronounced in old colonial English fashion with the accent on the first syllable — is itself Allah Din, religion of Allah. It changes to A'laddin — the stress is on the 'I' as north country English and Hollywood meet and mix.

A contemporary cartoon raises the transmutation stakes by representing the see-through, spectral genie in Scottish tartan kilt and sporran. Aladdin further translates into the Bengali-voiced Alauddin and Co., UK Sweetmeats, Brick Lane and Tooting Bec. We step into the scene of translations of Britain today, into the rough present of the 'dark migrations' — out of what might have seemed like a remote, abstruse linguistics debate between thinkers about the nature of translation.

The Western tourists have come and gone, bird-vanished as swiftly as they had arrived. Only their litter on Sri Lankan shores — photo bulbs, empty shampoo sachets, discarded bottles and jars, ballpoints, sweet containers, clapped-out batteries, cassettes, disposable cameras, throwaway plastics, Coca-Cola cans bobbing on the waves.... Picked up by some Sri Lankans they are crafted and wrought into objects of everyday use — colanders, graters, bowls, spoons and mugs, ladles. A treasure trove, an Aladdin's Cave of utensils hammered from tourist-junk. We have chanced upon an Aladdin's lamp made from local waste materials — tinned food can, light bulb, string wick, newsprint.

The tourists have flocked back delighted with these magical objects and utensils. They buy them, admiringly, affectionately. Overseen by the Institut für Auslandsbeziehungen in Stuttgart, Dr Grotheus's collection of such 'objects from foreign lands' went on exhibition-tour across Germany. It was requisitioned by the Sydney Biennale '93 — for a less formal, less museum style display. It was thus translated for the third time by being displayed as something between the ethnographic item, the avant-garde readymade and the everyday object. As the indeterminate object between Sri Lanka, Stuttgart, Sydney, the hybrid stands before us: beyond it, traces of untranslatable leftovers?

Where translation is understood as a process of 'carrying over' and simply in terms of 'transparency' it tends to encourage a superficial, if seductive, attitude to 'multicultural translation' as the immediate visibility of all elements of multicultural community to one another — even in the face of an adverse actuality that thwarts and distresses such an ideal at every turn. Dare we hold on to the ideal, however, for the value of its critical demand — a utopian horizon against which multiculturalism might be scanned, kept on its toes, and shown up for having fallen short of its own claims?

But to focus on untranslatability is not only to acknowledge from the start the impossibilities and limits of translation. It is to highlight the dimension of what gets lost in translation, what

Derek Jarman,
Blue, 1993

happens to be left over. Since what is gained in the translation tussle — elements of hybridity and difference — is so impressive, it is easy to slip into thinking of it as an outright overcoming of the untranslatable. The concept then begins to function as the mirror image of 'purity' with no less of the latter's triumphal overtone. It takes on an all too positive, optimistic ring billed as the new international visual Esperanto — a tellingly hunky-dory word, Steiner reminds us, that half-echoes the Spanish for hope.

What antidote for this drive towards becoming a reductive, one-dimensional term? A recoding would need to index hybridity as a site shot through and traced with the untranslatable which serves as its supplement and prop. The upshot of this is to dramatise the incomplete, unfixed nature of the category. We begin to see hybridity not so much as a self-standing, fixed term but as an interdependent one — changing and rechanging as it interacts with the aura of the untranslatable, with the remains and leftovers of the translation exercise. These need to be accounted for and acknowledged at every turn, for, to use Adorno's words, like blood stains in a fairytale, they cannot be rubbed off.

But can the untranslatable be voiced at all? How to articulate the leftover inexpressibles of translation? Is it perhaps to be glimpsed in a back-to-front crazy word, an image's shimmer, the flick of a gesture, the intimacies of voice, in listening to its silences — an attentiveness that opens on to an erotics and ethics of the other beyond its untranslatability? Having kicked off its sturdy walking shoes, my English is in danger of perhaps becoming too comfortably slippered at this point.

Lothar Baumgarten's installation *Imago Mundi* for the *Wall to Wall* show (Serpentine, London, 1994) stages the international space — quite literally reindexing it through a look at the codes, lens, optics and manuals of representation itself. Wherever we stand, wherever we position ourselves, we are not able to grasp the dispersed elements of the drifting continents. However acrobatically we twist, turn and contort ourselves to bring things into view, it only serves to make us aware of the limits and blindspots of the view and viewing.

Africa, Asia, Australia, Europe — no position permits a viewing without itself turning into the viewed. What prevails is the sense of watching as we are being watched, of someone looking over our shoulder as we look *l'autre l'ailleurs* — the other, elsewhere, everywhere and besides. The very transparency blocks off and shutters, occludes. We are unable to totalise this mapping of the world, each time something slips out of our grip. We grapple with the leftovers, the remainder of the untranslatable. How to signal this except perhaps through Derek Jarman's blank-screened *Blue* (1993) — *silent, throbbing.*

Sarat Maharaj

Notes

1. Jacques Derrida, *Dissemination*, 1981, pp. 71-72 and 'Des Tours des Babel' in *Difference in Translation*, Ithaca, 1985, pp. 165-207 and 209-48, in which the object of commentary is Walter Benjamin. 'The Task of the Translator' in *Illuminations*, New York, 1969, pp. 69-82.
2. Gayatri Spivak, 'The Politics of Translation' in *Outside in the Teaching Machine*, Routledge, New York, 1993, pp. 179-200.
3. 'The Congo is Flooding the Acropolis' in *Interrogating Identity*, Grey Art Gallery, New York University, 1991-92, pp. 13-42. Also A. R. Chakraborty, *Translational Linguistics of Ancient India*, Calcutta, 1976.
4. A. Kroker, M. Kroker & D. Cook, *Panic Encyclopedia*, London, 1989, p. 119.
5. Marcel Duchamp to Richard Hamilton (26.11.'60) from the Duchamp/Hamilton unpublished letters (1957-68).

First published in *Global Visions: Towards a New Internationalism in the Visual Arts*, Kala Press/inIVA, 1994

*Aladdin's
Neue Lampe,*
Sri Lanka

Modernity and Difference

A Conversation between Stuart Hall and Sarat Maharaj

Stuart Hall

As I think is true of all important terms in this kind of debate, it is best to deconstruct a term before you use it, or at least explain what you do not intend it to mean. There is one sense of the term 'translation' that I do not want to awaken, which is the notion that there is an original text and that all translations are then necessarily partial renderings of that original. They stand in relation to the original text as copies to origin. However, I'm really not interested in the notion of origin in that sense, because my position is that most original texts, when looked at closely, turn out to be translations themselves.

I regard translation as an unending process, a process without a beginning. Except in myth, there is no moment when cultures and identities emerge from nowhere, whole within themselves, perfectly self-sufficient, unrelated to anything outside of themselves and with boundaries which secure their space from outside intrusion. I do not think that either historically or conceptually we should think of cultures or identities or indeed texts in that way. Every text has a 'before-text', every identity has its pre-identities. I am not interested in the notion of translation in terms of rendering what has already been authentically and authoritatively fixed; what I want to do instead is to think of cultural practices as always involved in the process of translating.

Cultural processes do not have a pure beginning; they always begin with some irritant, some dirty or 'worldly' starting point, if I can call it that. When I say 'dirty', I mean that there is no pure moment of beginning; they are always already in flow and translation, therefore, is always from one idiom, language or ideolect into another. All languages have their own internal character, their own kind of ethos, their own space, and so it is therefore impossible to think of a perfect translation; no such thing exists. One has always to think of cultural production of any kind as a reworking, as inadequate to its foundations, as always lacking something. There is always something which is left out. There is always mistranslation because a translation can never be a perfect rendering from one space or one language to another. It is bound to be somewhat misunderstood, as we are all always misunderstood in every dialogue we undertake. There is no moment of dialogic relationship with an other which is perfectly understood by them in exactly the way intended by us, because translation is a mediation between two already constituting worlds. There is no perfect transparency.

So the notion of a perfect translation does not help us at all. What we usually think of as polarised between copying or mimicking on the one hand and the moment of pure creativity on the other are really two moments that are mutually constituting – they do not exist in a pure form. Pure creativity draws on something which is already there; it moves from one space to another and the creative act is that movement. It is not that I have thought of something or said something or produced something which has never been produced before – it is not the romantic notion of a pure start. Nor is it the notion of a pure finish, because every translation generates another. No-one reads a translation without thinking, 'I bet that's what the original really means. I bet I could express it better.'

One has to think of meaning as constituted by an infinite, incomplete series of translations. I think cultures are like that too, and so are identities. I think cultural production is like that and I am sure that texts are like that. In fact, the notion of 'cultural translation' is absolutely central to an understanding of this whole field. There are many people who have contributed to this particular notion of translation which I am trying to invoke, but I shall mention just three names as a way of orienting my argument: Walter Benjamin, Jacques Derrida and Mikhail Bakhtin.

Sarat Maharaj
Stuart has put the ideas across clearly with regard to cultural translation – I feel there is little more I could add, except simply to expand on what he has said and refer back to my essay on the untranslatable, since for me the search for translatability

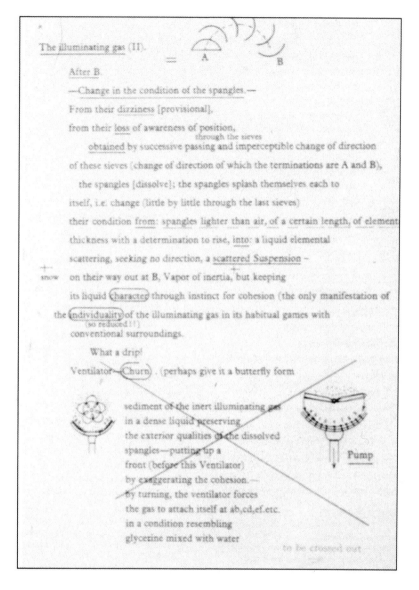

The illuminating gas (II). $=$ A B

After B.

—Change in the condition of the spangles.—

From their dizziness [provisional],

from their loss of awareness of position,
through the sieves
    obtained by successive passing and imperceptible change of direction

of these sieves (change of direction of which the terminations are A and B),

  the spangles [dissolve]; the spangles splash themselves each to

itself, i.e. change (little by little through the last sieves)

their condition from: spangles lighter than air, of a certain length, of element

thickness with a determination to rise, into: a liquid elemental

scattering, seeking no direction, a scattered Suspension –
+—
snow on their way out at B, Vapor of inertia, but keeping

its liquid character through instinct for cohesion (the only manifestation of

the individuality of the illuminating gas in its habitual games with
(so reduced !!)
conventional surroundings.

  What a drip!

Ventilator—Churn . (perhaps give it a butterfly form

    sediment of the inert illuminating gas
    in a dense liquid preserving
    the exterior qualities of the dissolved
    spangles—putting up a
    front (before this Ventilator)
    by exaggerating the cohesion.—
    by turning, the ventilator forces
    the gas to attach itself at ab,cd,ef,etc.
    in a condition resembling
    glycerine mixed with water

    Pump

to be crossed out

involves constantly bumping into and tussling with what is untranslatable. The names Stuart concluded with – Benjamin, Derrida and Bakhtin – are crucial from the point of view of a theoretical understanding of translation and of analysing what happens in the process: translation of identities, translation of cultures, translation of ethnicities. Whatever might be the case in hand, the point is that we are always in the process of translation – translation is not so much an exceptional moment in our lives but a condition of being and becoming.

Richard Hamilton, typographic translation of a page from Marcel Duchamp's *Green Box* notes, 1960

Against the three discursive and analytical commentators who have helped us so powerfully to comprehend the mechanisms of translations in the twentieth century, I would like to say that my own involvement begins in a much less grand, less theoretical way. It started quite simply through living in the Apartheid state which assumed to translate one and all 'ethnic and native' groups in the way it saw fit for modernity. We would be translated – our primordial, archaic features ironed out. We would be cleaned up, dusted down and given a voice in such a way that the Apartheid state could then speak to us and make us intelligible to itself. Growing up in such an environment irked all of us needless to say and the issue of translation was immediately both a violating political act and a political process of resistance.

Later on, during years of more solitary reflection on this question, I found two other thinkers helped me to delve deeper into the mechanisms of translation. They were James Joyce and Marcel Duchamp. They remain the figures with whom I have worked and tried to relate what I have understood about translation through that massive, sprawling, unreadable, untranslatable work, *Finnegans Wake,* and through the great untranslatables of Duchamp's notes and jottings for the *Large Glass – The Bride Stripped Bare by Her Bachelors, Even* (1911–1923). Richard Hamilton translated one batch of notes in 1960 as *The Green Box* and another bundle in 2000 as *The White Box.* These works served as instruments through which I tried to think about the stickiness of translation. While the analytical contributors to this question have largely focused on what can and can not be translated, I felt the practitioners Duchamp and Joyce also looked at and probed zones of the untranslatable. How do we live it? What does it mean to be in the experience of the untranslatable? Is it nonsense to talk of the untranslatable in these terms? But what kind of non-sense? Counter-signification, anti-meaning, what?

These reflections through Joyce and Duchamp strengthened the idea that although certain things can be translated in the domain of the linguistic, culture is far more than simply language and words. This produced in me a deep sense of the limits of words and language as the exclusive model through which we might think about cultural life and the translation of our everyday experience. With Joyce and Duchamp, there emerged, it seemed to me, a notion of translation which activates both the visual and the sonic. Beyond the *sense* of word and image are sounds which cannot be entirely drawn into the net of signification and cannot entirely be decoded and deciphered as meaning this, that or the other. These larger sonic pools – the penumbra of the untranslatable that shadow and smudge language and for which we have to venture beyond language – became an increasingly important area of interest in my thinking about cultural translation.

SH

There are a number of points that I would like to pick up on and develop from what Sarat has just said. One is about the notion of the untranslatable, that which escapes representation, or what is always left behind as a kind of resistant remainder. I, of course, accept the notion that everything cannot be translated. I think of the nature of the remainder in a slightly different way, which perhaps remains too confined within the linguistic domain and for that reason is, I think, somewhat limited. It has to do with how we understand meaning; whatever the medium in which it finds itself expressed, the notion of meaning always depends, in part, on what is not said, and on what is not represented, as part of meaning's constitutive outside. This is the notion, derived essentially from Ferdinand de Saussure, that one cannot know what it is that one means unless one also implicitly affirms or states what one does *not* mean – that every marked term or signifier implicates its unmarked 'other'.

It is a rather sobering thought to realise that this absent presence is true of all identities. I do not know of any identity which, in establishing what it is, does not, at the very same moment, implicitly declare what it is not, what has to be left out, excluded. In that sense, identities are always constructed through power, even though we do not like to think that they are, because no identity can include everyone. What would be the point of an identity which includes everyone? We understand 'sameness' only though difference, presence though what it 'lacks'. The whole point is to define what I and other people like me belong to; consequently an identity establishes itself by virtue of what is not and cannot be said to belong. To say or establish anything – any position, any presence, any meaning – one has to attend to what is outside the field of meaning and what cannot be expressed – its constitutive outside.

We are defined as much by what we are not as by what we are. The 'truth' of the Lacanian insight is that the subject is constructed across a 'lack', the self by its 'others'. This for me is an
40 absolutely fundamental point, because it implies that, within

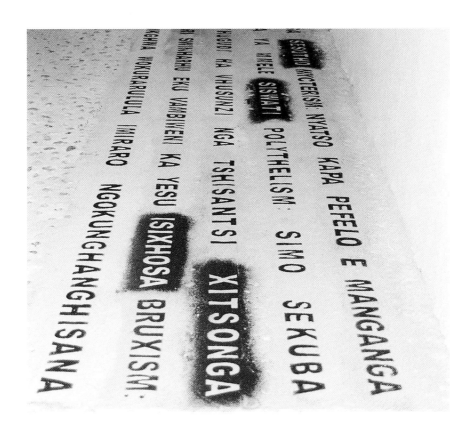

Willem
Boshoff,
*Writing in
the Sand*
(detail),
2000

ourselves, within the terms of a meaning, we are always
inadequate. We cannot complete ourselves. We are always open to
that which is other or different from ourselves, which we cannot
encapsulate into ourselves, draw into our field of meaning or
representation. This notion of a lack has psychoanalytic Lacanian
echoes, but I do not want to get into that today. However, I do
not think that you could talk about an identity without talking
about what an identity lacks – difference. This is very important
because it is the point at which one recognises that one can only
be constituted through the other, through what is different.
Difference, therefore, is not something that is opposed to
identity; instead it is absolutely essential to it. You cannot talk
about the identity of a set of terms without talking about how
they are different from what that set of terms does not include.
So the question of difference then does, for me, emerge from
what Sarat said about the untranslatable.

If I want to say something, I have to form a statement of
some kind, which is true of whatever medium I am using.
There is always a kind of closure to that, because I have not

41

finished saying anything until I stop. In language, that stop
or closure is both necessary and arbitrary. It is necessary
because the thought cannot be completed until you frame it,
but the frame is completely arbitrary because the moment
somebody else responds to that statement, the frame is
reopened – your previous statement (totalisation) is completely
detotalised. My perfectly finished thought stops and somebody
else, by taking up the thread and elaborating it in a new
direction, implicitly says, 'Of course that's not quite so.' So
we move from arbitrary closure to movement to other closures,
which is how dialogue – the dialogic – works. I think of any
text, sentence or work as a moment of arbitrary closure in
what I call the infinite flow of meaning – the infinite semiosis
of language. Thus, as Bakhtin argues, no speech is wholly my
own, but is sustained in the passage of meaning between
speakers (the metaphor here is linguistic but applies also to
the visual field).

Isaac Julien,
Vagabondia,
2000

Any statement which has a meaning for another human being is
therefore grounded in more than what it says – its excess – but is
also less than what you want it to say; it is the result of
arbitrary closure. It is not a completely full, self-present
statement of everything, because if it was, history and meaning
would end; it would give up the ghost. It would say, in effect,
'OK, that's the sentence we've all been trying to say since the
year dot and, now you've said it, there's nowhere else to go.'

The supposedly finished statement is instantly overridden by that
which it cannot say, that which it has not said, that which it
cannot bring into representation. Meaning – not cognitive
meaning only, but anything that somebody else will get
something out of – is therefore always constituted in the
interplay between excess and lack. And that is another way of
thinking about what is *not* and can never be inside
representation – the untranslatable.

I am interested in asking Sarat whether what he means by the untranslatable, which in a sense gives power to the images and the language he is talking about, is the same as, or different from, or close to what I have just said about what has to be left out of representation. I am strongly aware that my argument is grounded in a conception of language and is using the linguistic as a kind of master model of meaning, which is something that I do not mean to impose.

SM
I think that Stuart has, as usual, lucidly presented how one would think of the untranslatable if one were to proceed with the linguistic model as a master model. Language has served in most of our thinking about cultural translation and I suppose that translation itself seems to be so tied up with words, translating from one language to the other. Those of us who come from areas that also involve image and sound have therefore had to really sit up and think about second-round translation – the translation of image to image, image to sound, or image to word – which is not entirely served by the linguistic model.

I feel what Stuart has presented is absolutely central to an understanding of identity and difference, difference that cannot be stopped and difference that continuously writes itself in the way Duchamp speaks of writing 'in the infinitive'. Imagine something that could never be written in 'stationary verbs' that give a standstiff account of where one is, but is instead written 'in the infinitive', forever suggesting potential movement out of itself into a future that is, as yet, not described, nor defined, nor in any way pictured. Even within linguistic terms, if I think of translation as being an act in the infinitive mood, then I get close to Stuart's notion of perpetual translation in which no sooner you feel you have fixed an identity, you have to translate it again and again and again.

This sometimes produces the effect of saying that identity is a series of negations, of saying this is not what it is, this is not what I mean, this is not how I see it. In fact, there has a been a line of thinking, particularly in twentieth-century music and visual arts, which can be traced back to the famous words uttered by the Buddha. Asked to describe what is the essence of things, what is identity, he simply answered with three words which have reverberated throughout the twentieth-century avant-garde. He replied, in Sanskrit, '*Neti, neti, neti*', meaning, 44 'Not this, not that, not this'. Having heard these words, some

Thomas
Hirschhorn,
*Deleuze
Monument:
La Beauté*,
Champfleury,
Avignon,
2000

felt that this was extreme mystification and were exasperated by this kind of answering. Later, commentators, particularly in the Indian school of philosophy called the Nyaya-Vaisesika, went on to elaborate thinking in terms of such negatives. They stopped trying to define what we are, as though one could hold one's identity, one's sense of self in the palm of one's hand. When they did try to, they did so in a very knowing way, conscious that what they said would be translated, rephrased, recast again. So those would be my notations to Stuart's clear account of the linguistic model.

I have tried to struggle with the notion of the untranslatable as that area that is simply the leftover – Stuart mentioned the term remainder – the 'leftover-dross' in the act of translation. When one language, one experience, one visual or retinal regime gets translated into another, it has to be re-jigged to fit into the system of thinking of the other and something is 'left out'. This remainder – at least this is what logically appears when you analyse translation – inhabits the space of the untranslatable, a fog that persists no matter how much in everyday life we feel we overcome the untranslatable and manage to thrash out a ground of crystal-clear communication for ourselves. In some instances, 45 artists have gone on to say that translation – even from one set of words to another – demands picturing or somehow seeing what is left. The remainder which cannot be put into words might be something you can visualise or something that can be suggested through sonic stuff, through 'sounding of that difference' as a kind of turbulence, as a cloud of disturbance around clear-cut linguistic meaning.

In the more political sense, I understand the untranslatable to mean that which resists translation – in the sense that it refuses the state's ability to translate and slot a person into a set category of difference. When a government attempts to fix a person into a difference-box and then treats him or her according to a policy or programme of diversity, I call this pigeon-holing *multicultural managerialism*. In the light of my concern about that managerialism and fixing of difference, I have tried to explore beyond the linguistic model to understand the untranslatable not simply as a place of resistance or turbulence or perturbation, but as one of elusive liquidity – in Duchamp's and Bergson's lingo, as a matter of 'passages' rather than 'stoppages'.

SH

I think we ought to go straight on, as Sarat has done, and take these ideas into the political arena. There is a great deal of turbulence today when two cultures, two identities, two texts meet in the same space. The greater the turbulence that is created, the more likely it is that managerialism steps in, because everybody expects to define how two incommensurable texts should become more like one another, or at any rate occupy discrete spaces which can be identified, regulated and organised. They want them to remain sufficiently stable and fixed, to achieve a kind of closed system, in which you trade a bit of your differences for a bit of mine and so on. And now I suppose we ought to ask what is wrong with this? Is it not a laudable, liberal, tolerant way of managing these difficult situations? Are you really inviting societies – which are increasingly obliged to try to make a life in which these different cultures and texts join together and occupy the same space – to accept two facts: firstly, that the maps of difference will never settle down in a way which can be predictable, administered by policy, or regulated in a rational way; and, secondly, that an element of the disturbance of the untranslatable will always be part of this encounter? I do not think one can duck the fact that these are not just textual questions, but they are also
46 closely interwoven with social questions.

SM

The move away from the linguistic model to some extent was demanded by my anxiety about cultural translation becoming a purely textual issue, becoming purely commentaries upon texts upon texts. There is a risk that we trap ourselves perfecting the system of conceptualisation, never breaking out to connect with the streaming practices and processes of everyday life. That *conductivity* is what I have tried to address in speaking of the untranslatable through a series of scenarios of 'juxta-linear translation', of 'transubstantiation', or of 'currency-rate translation'; there are various other models of translation which I have tried to develop around the master notion. I think the question Stuart has posed is an important and difficult one. I do not think I have an absolute answer. Instead I see the paradoxes and the collision courses that one enters into in this sort of analysis — between the political necessity of wrapping up the flow and the need for 'stoppages' and for keeping things 'in the infinitive', for 'passages'.

I can only but support and back the liberal democracies in their attempt to want to grapple with difference. I see that as an extremely important, creative advance on the position that existed twenty years ago, or even more recently, when difference was consigned to invisibility. 'Difference' was seen as something that was a pre-modern hangover that would have to be ironed out in a process of assimilation, of being rendered part of the modern world. This assumption that difference is simply a problem that will be overcome when the state inducts the other, the different and the diverse into a notion of sameness and modernity is now being challenged by fresh thinking in the liberal democracies. The European Union, in particular, with its concerted state policies of cultural diversity, has had to tackle the presence of difference which cannot be assimilated and treated as though it is simply an archaic, obsolete element that, given time, will modernise and also begin shopping at Safeway. This shift has led to a concern with wanting to order difference and, in the better sense of the term, to 'manage' it.

At the same time, I see — involved as a dialectic within this attempt to order, to address, to create space for difference — elements marked by the Apartheid state's attempt to regulate difference. This attempt at regulation at the heart of addressing difference worries me. I feel we have to counter it by a sense of a turbulent process vis-à-vis difference, to look at its

Nasrin Tabatabai, *The Weaver-bird*, 2000

disturbances and the way it trips up the all-too-settled frame which the state – or government or European Union – policies establish for us and in which we are expected to operate as functions and factors of difference. I see a political procedure – stoppages – and I see a philosophical, experiential analysis – passages – but I do not think these are squareable. In my mind and my work, they do not run together; there is an element of their being always out of synch. Therefore I shall go back to say that I do not have an absolute answer to this.

SH

I agree with much of what you say, but I want to explore it further. First of all, I acknowledge the advances which have been made by liberal democracies in exploring what would be involved in coming to terms with difference. I am sure, however, that you would want me to raise a warning note that this is so far an extremely uneven and incomplete process; there are plenty of areas of the liberal democratic world which are still perfectly prepared to override or deny difference, or to manage it in a very different way.

In this context, it is worth identifying with one of the most difficult things to comprehend nowadays about this society – the absolute coincidence of multiculturalism and racism. Far from being the opposite ends of a pole so that one can trade the rise of one against the decline of the other, it seems to be absolutely dead central to society that both multiculturalism and racism are increasing at one and the same time. This is partly because the society we are talking about is not in any sense unified around any of these projects. Some people think multiculturalism is wonderful and they can not imagine life without it. They are usually young and they mainly live in London. Others think they cannot do anything about the creeping multicultural drift, but they hope that it will stay in the urban centres and, if they move to the country, it will not try to marry their daughters. Yet others cannot stand the sight of it. They are driven completely crazy by the very idea of a multicultural Britain and a minority of those will go so far as to stick knives into it and beat it over the head with a table leg if they come across it. It is a very confused picture. We could hardly have expected anything different from a society like Britain which has been constituted as a closed culturally homogeneous entity (although Britain has never been a mono-cultural entity in its life, despite its official story of itself). The fact that some parts of society are now willing, tentatively, to ask the question of how differences are to be lived is thus a very important step.

Personally, however, I think that the process could easily be reversed; I do not think that it is by any means secure, even in Europe. Improvements seem to have been made on three bases. Firstly, that of greater and greater assimilation – or where the differences become so minor that they no longer matter very much. If they do not trouble you very much, if they are kept in private and only occur behind closed doors, or in those parts of the city which normal folks do not visit, if they are not 'in your face', then they are much easier to accept. This is a pacified form of difference and here the untranslatable is absolutely crucial it seems, because I feel not a conscious, so much as an unconscious, resistance to giving in to assimilation in that way. Secondly, there was a very important moment in liberal democracy, in the 1970s I think, when the dream of some perfect assimilation, in which all differences would be obliterated into a colour-free universe, died a death. I do not think anybody thinks that dream is going to be revived, which is a kind of acknowledgment that people feel some things so deeply that they are not going to let them be translated out of existence. They are not going to have them commodified or regulated or managed. The third issue is how we begin to think about or deal with the turbulence that you talked about, the unpredictable nature or raw experience of encountering difference that will not go away, because it is too deeply embedded to be wished away.

Politically, we have to begin to think in terms of a democratic project which is an argument, a real battle or struggle – an agonistic form of democratic dialogue – which is the absolute reverse of everybody going to the polling booth every five years and voting for X or Y. A row has to happen, as people trade away the things which do not matter and get down to those irreducible points where they can say, 'My route into modernity is different from yours, and that constitutes me as a different kind of person. It constitutes my life as a different project from yours.' Is the only response to difference that we must eat one another? Or is there some way of learning to live *with* difference.

I have been involved this week in the aftermath of the commission on the Future of a Multi-Ethnic Britain, during which people have said to me that I should be proud to be British. There is only one question in response to that: which British? There are many things about Britain that I am proud of. And then there are all the bits of Britishness which I absorbed directly and intravenously at about the age of two months. I came to England thinking that every flower was a daffodil, because the Romantic poets had been injected directly into my bloodstream; I could hardly name a Jamaican flower and to discover that all English flowers were not daffodils was really rather surprising. So, yes, of course there are some senses in which I am 'British'. And yet I cannot relate to the British Empire in the same way that a native English person does. I never will, so either that is the end of the conversation or we have to find some way of getting beyond that. It is not going to be an easy dialogue and it has to recognise my own willingness to trade the specificity of what is different about the routes by which I come to the present and to modernity and the routes by which they have come to modernity. This is an ineradicable, an untranslatable kind of difference, which the Home Secretary and the programmes for 'cultural diversity' do not want to hear about. So, unfortunately, we have got to go on trying to make the translation as effective as possible and yet also be prepared for the thing to explode in our face because of what is not tradable, what is not manageable, what remains stubbornly outside the field of representational translatability.

Gilane Tawadros
I would like to ask a pragmatic question about how you deal with the two elements of untranslatability. On the one hand there is a

50

resistance to untranslatability and there exists a point at which you have to define what cannot be negotiated, what is the final border. How does that work? How can that operate? How can one imagine that within the space of everyday life, within the political domain, whether that be as a citizen or in terms of governance? On the other hand, there is a desire for completeness which sits opposite or beneath that untranslatability. It is the desire for that perfect translation and to be able to square that circle which is constantly being articulated in one way or another.

SH

The difference which is untranslatable is not a fixed and essential thing; it is itself the product of a translation and is itself, always, in motion. It is not as though it is and will always be there and that nothing will ever break into it. It is not like that. The moment when one is required to enter some common space is the point at which the recognition of difference is absolutely central, because every real negotiation depends on the recognition of its limits. At the same time, the recognition of similarity is also important, because similarity is the horizontal to the vertical of difference. Nothing is pure difference; there is no essentialised difference. Difference remains, but not fixed immutably by its origins, not immured in an unchanging 'tradition', because it is open to movement and located within other dimensions which cut across that, which laterally connect you with other people.

I no longer believe in some abstract universal set of values that you can import into the conversation to trump every other particular, such as your Egyptianness, his South Africanness, my Caribbeanness. Nor do I subscribe to a view of human rights or universal human values which have nothing to do with the own particular lives that we have lived. Far from it. I think the only way in which people who are different could come to constitute a common conversation is by recognising the inadequacy of each of our positions as well as what is not translatable. The moment you take the radical inadequacy, the 'lack', of your own position into account, there is a broadening, a widening, an ethical reach for that which is different from you but which also constitutes you – the reach or the other. It is an ethical acknowledgment of our own incompleteness and it is only in that space that people can begin to trade. That is the point where negotiation becomes feasible, but only if the two elements are entering as equal partners to the trade, as equal partners to the dialogue. It cannot be your conversation into which I am fitting or your idiom which I have to learn.

I do not want to talk about the stubbornness and the rawness of what we are calling the untranslatable as if it is some fixed, originary foundational point. That is not the way to think about it. Whatever moment you cut into it, the positions will be in different spaces, located differently in relation to one another. You therefore have to think both about what people will not give up and what might frame that dialogue in such a way that people can participate equally in working out some future which includes them all and which acknowledges the lack which each of us has in our need for recognition from the other. This is what Ernesto Laclau calls the universal, not as something from outer space which trumps every particular, but an incomplete horizon reached for from within each inadequate particular.

SM

I think it is really important that Stuart has emphasised the fact that we are not speaking of difference as though it were always present as a primordial space – as though the untranslatable were the primordial penumbra of the translated. We face this with regard to the relationship between the global and the local too; there is the assumption that somehow the global is bad and then there is this primordial good called the local that we must somehow hold on to as the point of resistance. It is often overlooked that the local is as much produced by the processes of the global and therefore we have a far more complicated, tricky relationship between the local and global to think through.

The same is true with the translatable and the untranslatable, which is a produced effect of the act and process of translation. It is shifting, fugitive, not easy to pinpoint, define and work out how to deal with, which is what I feel the liberal democratic state tries to do. A bunch of untranslatable immigrants arrive and the state says, 'What do we do with them? How do we translate them?' Not unlike how the Apartheid state reacted to untranslatable archaic natives, immigrants, indentured labourers, whatever the case was, and set about translating them. In that process difference is treated in the banal form that Stuart was referring to, in which everything seems to be 'sorted', to use a colloquialism, and organised and given its place. This display of cultural diversity becomes an extension of cultural tourism.

Qiu Zhijie,
*Elysium:
Ornament
from the
West, 1999*

'Yuanmingyuan was the regius gardens of Qing dynasty famous of its European style, but it was burned by English and France aggressor in 19th century. Today it is the most important traveled landscape and regarded as the symbol of patriotism education.'

'The architectural surbase antefix and encrust with Romanize style is the most fashion window dressing in chinese family since 1990th.'

'In the Buddhism sutra *A Mi Tou Jing*, the western is pictured as an ellysium called *Pure Land*, which everybody hopes to resurrection there.'

In the West, we see not only terrible waves of xenophobia, but also greater waves of xenophilia at the same time – a baffling thing about the current, contemporary situation. Cultural tourism tends to promote a strong sense of wanting to be with the other – desiring the different, the foreign, the strange in pre-digested terms – to the extent that we can visit Jamaica and yet not visit Jamaica, we can visit India and yet not visit it, South Africa and yet not quite visit it. We consume the country as a series of markers of difference, which are given to us as packets and packages of experience of the other. They are just different enough to make a good holiday without too many moments of turbulence. The turbulence I speak of concerns the sense of freefall and melt-down of ethical engagement with difference, which goes beyond its packaged, manicured version as the experience of curious, titillating difference sifted down to diversity. The production of cultural tourism is precisely the spectacular condition of the contemporary world engendering a kind of xenophilia, which the liberal democratic state tends to orchestrate through programmes of diversity. Important as these programmes are in grappling with difference, they screen engagement with difference, producing, as Stuart reminds us, those situations in which you are likely to get your head bashed in or remain the object of murder because you represent troubling difference. You are cast as a remainder that cannot be entertained, retussled with, and therefore a difference that has to be violated.

How do we deal with difference without fixing it as a version of ourselves? How do we deal with difference without entirely reducing it to the terms and the categories of our own language? I know we have to deal with it in the social domain, in the everyday domain and in political terms. But I question whether language itself can deal with difference in any fundamental sense. Is language not always subject to a self-deception? It is not able to face the fact that it has demolished the other in some way, recomposed it in terms of its own linguistic competency and grammar regime. This act of violation at the heart of language, at the heart of conceiving the other, leads me to look for para-linguistic ways of engaging the other – drawing it into the ethical encounter with difference. I suppose that I am prepared to say that there is a *xenocidal* drive in language; it murders the 'foreign' other, it violates the other to such an extent that it brings to the fore only what it can deal with in its terms – in terms of its own epistemic frame. Now this might be a slightly pessimistic, somewhat downbeat view of language, but I feel that it might help us to explore the complicated cultural situation in the liberal democracies, where we see an advance in dealing with difference, accompanied by some of the most atrocious forms of violation of difference and diversity. And I am asking if this knotted complexity is tackled at all in the forms of language we have?

SH

My immediate response is that this is not best thought of in terms of language versus other media of expression. Whatever the medium, unless it is used in such a way as not simply to reproduce existing categories and orders, it will have this violating effect of closure on the other and cause rejection. This may have something to do with modernism, because it is only in and after modernism that languages – both visual and verbal languages of representation – have been broken up and fractured in terms of their ability to reproduce the world directly, in some literal way. It is only when language is 'in that break' that you can get disturbance into the language itself and, at that point, to put it crudely, Joyce can do as good a job, and is doing rather the same job, as Duchamp. Within their spheres – the linguistic and the visual – they are both operating in such a way that the objects they constitute, whatever the medium, no longer fit perfectly within an already existing system of reference and meaning; the means themselves disturb and unsettle or subvert any attempt to translate things back into their originals in a seamless way.

I would prefer to talk therefore in terms of what is done with *language*, in the broader sense, or the means of representation of whatever one is talking about, rather than speaking of the linguistic versus the visual. I do not deny that the linguistic, in the narrower sense, has been a powerful carrier in Western culture of the cognitive and the conceptual, and so it is a more difficult model to apply to the visual field. However, I do not think that the linguistic and visual are mutually exclusive. Or, to put it the other way, a lot of visual work seems to me thinkable within the model of what we may call 'the linguistic' or 'the discursive' turn.

SM

That was not quite what I intended – I am not trying to pit visual against verbal. I could not, at any rate, do so given my equal involvement with Joyce and Duchamp. Both, however, do seriously distress the idea that all meaning is discursive. I am keen, however, to press home the difficulties faced with the linguistic-discursive because I do feel other domains, semantic or otherwise – the visual-sonic – tend to be left out of the discussion of the ethical encounter with difference.

Joyce often tips over the verbal into the visual. Duchamp moves away from the retinal, making the optical into the conceptual as much as, in another about-turn, he makes us look at text as image, as 'visible grammar'. Both play out convoluted verbal-visual-sonic interactions and semantic fissions. My aim, therefore, is not, as suggested by a member of the audience, to 'discredit' the linguistic. 'Discredit' is quite off the mark and, at any rate, it is too strong a word – this is England! The aim is rather to put pressure on the conceptual-discursive not so much with a counter-linguistic but with a para-linguistic – not so much with its binary opposite as with a modality that goes with, around, through and beyond the linguistic. To adapt Duchamp, a 4-D translation 'in the infinitive' – a 'circum-hyper-hypo-translation'.

Modernity and Difference, a talk organised by inIVA, took place at the Lux Centre, Hoxton, London, on 25 October 2000

Pavel Braila,
Recalling
Events, 2000

Biographies

Professor Stuart Hall
was born in Jamaica in 1932. He came to England in 1951 to study as a Rhodes Scholar at Merton College, Oxford, and has lived in Britain ever since. He was the first editor of *New Left Review* and was active in the peace movement and anti-racist work in the 1960s and 1970s. He was a secondary school teacher in London and taught media studies at Chelsea College, University of London. In 1964, he went to Birmingham University to help establish the Centre for Cultural Studies and was Research Fellow, and then Director, of the Centre until 1979, when he went as Professor of Sociology to the Open University. He retired in 1997. He is now Emeritus Professor of Sociology at the Open University and currently Visiting Professor at Goldsmiths College, University of London. He chairs the boards of inIVA and Autograph, the Association of Black Photographers. He is married with two children.

Stuart Hall has written and broadcast extensively over the years in cultural studies; on the media and visual representation; on race, ethnicity and cultural identity; on contemporary politics, race and urban crime; and on critical social and cultural theory.

Professor Sarat Maharaj
was born in Durban, South Africa, and educated at the University of South Africa, Durban (for Blacks of Indian Origin). He was given residency in the United Kingdom in 1976 under the Geneva Convention for Refugees and completed his PhD on 'The Dialectic of Modernism and Mass Culture: Studies in Postwar British Art' at the University of Reading. He is a member of the boards of inIVA, Tate Britain and the Gate Foundation, Amsterdam, and on the advisory board of *Third Text*. He is also co-curator of *Documenta XI*.

Sarat Maharaj is Professor of Art History and Theory at Goldsmiths College, University of London; Research Fellow at Jan Van Eyck Akademie, Maastricht; and the first Rudolf Arnheim Professor of Art History at Humboldt University, Berlin. He has lectured and published throughout the world on cultural translation and difference. He is an authority on the work of Richard Hamilton, Marcel Duchamp and James Joyce and his experimental writings include textiles art, sound work (Xeno-sonics) and visual theory constructions (Monkeydoodle).

Select Bibliography

Stuart Hall, 'Cultural Identity and Diaspora', in *Identity: Community, Culture, Difference*, edited by Jonathan Rutherford, Lawrence & Wishart, 1990

Stuart Hall, 'The Question of Cultural Identity', in *Modernity and its Futures*, edited by Stuart Hall et al., Polity Press and the Open University, 1992

Stuart Hall, 'New Ethnicities' and 'What is this "Black" in Black Popular Culture?', both reprinted in *Stuart Hall: Critical Dialogues in Cultural Studies*, edited by David Morley and Kuan-Hsing Chen, Routledge, 1996

Stuart Hall, 'Minimal Selves', in *Black British Cultural Studies*, edited by Houston A. Baker et al., University of Chicago Press, 1996

Stuart Hall, 'When Was the Post-Colonial?', in *The Post-Colonial Question: Common Skies, Divided Horizons*, edited by Iain Chambers and Lidia Curti, Routledge, 1996

Stuart Hall and Paul du Gay, *Questions of Cultural Identity*, Sage, 1996

Stuart Hall, 'The Work of Representation' and 'The Spectacle of the Other', in *Representation*, edited by

Stuart Hall, Sage and the Open University, 1997

Stuart Hall, 'Thinking the Diaspora', in *Small Axe*, no. 6, 1999

Stuart Hall, 'The Multicultural Question', in *Un/Settled Multiculturalisms*, edited by Barnor Hesse, Zed Books, 2000

Sarat Maharaj, 'The Congo is Flooding the Acropolis. Black Art and Orders of Difference' in *Interrogating Identity*, New York University, Grey Art Gallery and Study Centre, 1991

Sarat Maharaj, 'A Liquid Elemental Scattering: Marcel Duchamp and Richard Hamilton' in *Richard Hamilton*, Tate Gallery Publications, 1992

Sarat Maharaj, *Domestic Borderations of Today's Homes, Tomorrow's Worlds*, in *Richard Hamilton: XLV Biennale di Venezia, British Pavilion*, British Council, 1993

Sarat Maharaj, 'Perfidious Fidelity: The Untranslatability of the Other' in *Global Visions*, edited by Jean Fisher, Kala Press/inIVA, 1994

Sarat Maharaj, 'A Monster of Veracity, a Crystalline Transubstantiation...:

Typo-Translating Marcel Duchamp's Green Box' in *The Duchamp Effect*, edited by M. Dixon, MIT, 1996

Sarat Maharaj, 'A Falsemeaning Adamelegy: Artisanal Signatures of Difference after Gutenberg' in JURASSIC *Technologies Revenant*, edited by Lynne Cooke, 10th Biennale of Sydney, 1996

Sarat Maharaj, 'Extra-Rapid Delay: Visual Art and Cultural Difference' in *Reinventing Britain*, video by the British Council and website

Sarat Maharaj, 'Dislocutions: Interim Entries for a *dictionnaire élémentaire* on Cultural Translation' in *Reverberations*, edited by Jean Fisher, Jan Van Eyck Akademie, 2000

Sarat Maharaj, '*Avidya*: Non-Knowledge Production in the Visual Arts Field' in *Education. Information. Entertainment*, edited by Ute Meta Bauer, Vienna, 2001

Sarat Maharaj, *Work in Pregross*, inIVA, forthcoming

Sarat Maharaj, *A Strife of Tongues: Richard Hamilton/Marcel Duchamp/James Joyce*, Typosophic Society, forthcoming

Illustration Credits

Every effort has been made to trace all copyright holders, but if any have inadvertently been overlooked, the publisher will be pleased to make the necessary arrangements at the first opportunity.

p. 6
Courtesy of *Revelation Magazine*/Lyndon Douglas

p. 10
Courtesy of the artist
© Tate London, 2001
'I was informed by the Tate Gallery in London that my *painting Two Saints in a Landscape* is the first painting they have in their collection that was ever done in the medium called acrylics, or PolyVinylAcetate (PVA) as it was then known in the 1960s.' – F.N. Souza

p. 15
Suspended disk
Collection of the artist's estate
Photo: Li Yuan-chia

p. 17
Sand, tissue paper and acrylic on canvas, 200 x 300 cm
Courtesy of the artist

p. 20
Collection of the artist
Photo: Guy Brett

p. 23
Courtesy of the artist

pp. 24-25
Oil on canvas, 132 x 208 cm
Private collection
Reproduced by kind permission of Eve Williams
Photo: Edward Woodman

p. 28
Courtesy of the artist
Photo: Zarina Bhimji

p. 29
Installation shot at *Parisien(ne)s*, Camden Arts Centre, London
Photo: Edward Woodman

p. 32
Courtesy Basilisk Communications

p. 35
Courtesy of the Institut für Auslandsbeziehungen, Stuttgart
Photo: Dr Grotheus

p. 38
Courtesy of the artist

p.41
Willem Boshoff, *Writing in the Sand*, 2000
Installation.Text stencilled on to the floor in sand found at the exhibition site. 6 x 11.5m
Courtesy of the artist
'The homage rendered by *Writing in the Sand* to South Africa's survivor languages is a precarious one. The advent of European influence in our land has already witnessed, if not indeed brought about, the extinction or near demise of smaller languages like San, Khoisan, Khoekhoen, Nama and Griqua. I write in the sand because it is an unstable medium and is easily disturbed. Writing in sandy places is easily damaged and extirpated by water and wind. My work deals primarily with this loss. It points at an abject extinction of a people's collective myth when they no longer share it by word of mouth. It also hints at the fugitive nature of information in cyberspace and the loss of smaller languages due to the dominance of superlanguages in their all-out attempt to be heard clearly in a world where everyone tries to shout at their loudest....'
'Language is a precious thing. Our mother only begins to give birth to us by bringing our physical body into the world. Thereafter she and other mentors close to us give birth to our customs, culture and religion, and, most importantly, to our language. We speak for very good reason of a "mother tongue". A comforting cloak of language covers us within our respective groups. It unites and divides us. It heartens and enrages us. When we share our mother tongue with others who

also speak it, we can
be as poetic, as
comprehensive, as
spellbinding and as
persuasive as the best of
speakers in any of the
world's major languages.'
- Willem Boshoff
This text is published in
full in the catalogue for
the Seventh Havana
Biennial, *Séptima Bienal
de la Habana* (Art for the
World, Geneva, 2000).

pp. 42–43
Double screen 16mm colour
film transferred to DVD
Courtesy of the artist

p. 45
Courtesy of the artist
Photo: Thomas Hirschhorn

p. 48
Courtesy of the artist
Photo © B. Goedewaagen

p. 53
Film still. Courtesy of the
artist

p. 57
Film still. Courtesy of the
artist

Acknowledgments

Jacques Bayle
Maria Beddoes
Guy Brett
Paul Khera
Scott Lee Cash
The Lux Centre
James Mackay
Rohini Malik
Peter Mayers
Revelation Magazine
Tate Gallery
Paul Thurlow
Yvonne van de Griendt
Mark Wayman
Eve Williams

Stuart Hall:
My thanks to David Bailey,
Homi Bhabha, Paul Gilroy,
Catherine Hall, Isaac
Julien, Mark Nash, Mark
Sealy and Gilane Tawadros
for helping me, in various
ways, to think more
productively about these
questions.

Sarat Maharaj:
My thanks to Richard
Hamilton, Rita Donagh,
Ecke Bonk, Jackie Monnier
and the late Madame Tini
Duchamp for the Duchamp
knowledge. Thanks to
Goldsmiths College's
'Joyce-Duchamp-Hamilton'
students for help in
developing the translation
idea. Special thanks
to Gilane Tawadros and
Sarah Campbell for their
efforts in getting this
text published.

Other Titles in the Series

Annotations 1
Mixed Belongings and
Unspecified Destinations
Edited by Nikos
Papastergiadis
80 pages,
17 illustrations,
1996

ISBN 1 899846 09 3

Annotations 2
Sonia Boyce:
Performance
Edited by Mark Crinson
64 pages,
26 illustrations,
11 in colour,
1998

ISBN 1 899846 15 8

Annotations 3
Frequencies:
Investigations into
Culture, History and
Technology
Edited by Melanie Keen
88 pages, 30 illustrations,
1998

ISBN 1 899846 16 6

Annotations 4
Steve Ouditt:
Creole In-Site
Edited by Gilane Tawadros
72 pages,
15 illustrations,
6 in colour,
1998

ISBN 1 899846 18 2

Annotations 5
Run Through the Jungle:
Selected Writings by
Eddie Chambers
Edited by Gilane Tawadros
and Victoria Clarke
140 pages,
19 illustrations,
1999

ISBN 1 899846 20 4

For further information
about inIVA titles, please
contact:
inIVA
6-8 Standard Place
Rivington Street
London EC2A 3BE
Tel: +44 20 7729 9616
Fax: +44 20 7729 9509
E-mail: institute@iniva.org
www.iniva.org